THE RICH DADDY
Unlocking Financial Freedom and
Creating a Legacy of Wealth

DANNY J.BAYS

COPYRIGHT

TABLE OF CONTENT

CHAPTER 10
The Balanced wealth

INTRODUCTION

In this chapter, we are introduced to John,the central protagonist of our story.Meet John, a remarkable individual who embodies the perfect blend of a successful entrepreneur and a loving father. With an unwavering determination and a compassionate heart, John has managed to create an extraordinary life for himself and those around him.

As an entrepreneur, John possesses a brilliant mind and an innovative spirit. He has always been driven by his passion for creating something meaningful and impactful. With his keen business acumen and a knack for identifying opportunities, he has established several successful ventures that have garnered both financial prosperity and admiration from his peers. John's entrepreneurial journey has been marked by his ability to think outside the box, taking risks when necessary, and consistently pushing boundaries to achieve greatness. However, John's success as an entrepreneur never overshadows his most cherished role as a father. Above all else, he values his family and cherishes every moment spent with his children. John is a devoted and attentive father, always prioritizing the well-being and happiness of his kids. He actively participates in their lives, engaging in activities that foster their growth and providing a nurturing environment for them to flourish.

CHAPTER 1

The Awakening.

Introduction to the protagonist, John, a middle-aged man struggling with financial difficulties.

The turning point in John's life when he decides to change his financial situation for the better.

John's realization that becoming a rich and successful person will positively impact his family's future.

Introduction: The opening chapter of "The Rich Daddy" introduces the protagonist, John, a middle-aged man who finds himself in a challenging financial situation. John has been working hard all his life, yet he struggles to make ends meet, constantly living paycheck to paycheck. He is burdened by debts, unable to provide his family with the financial security he desires.

The Struggle: John's financial struggles have taken a toll on him emotionally and strained his relationships. He often feels stressed, anxious, and frustrated. One day, as he sits down to pay bills, he realizes that he can no longer continue living this way. He experiences a moment of profound realization—a wake-up call that prompts him to take control of his financial destiny.

The Turning Point: John recognizes that he needs to change his financial situation not just for himself but also for the sake of his family's future. He realizes that he wants to be a role model for his children, teaching them the value of financial responsibility and providing them with a better life. This turning point sparks a determination within John to seek knowledge and take action.

Research and Reflection: Following his awakening, John embarks on a journey of self-education. He starts reading books, attending seminars, and exploring online resources to gain a deeper understanding of personal finance and wealth creation. He reflects on his past financial decisions and identifies the patterns and behaviors that have led him to his current circumstances.

The Mindset Shift: Through his research and reflection, John begins to recognize the importance of mindset in achieving financial success. He realizes that his negative beliefs and limited thinking have held him back from reaching his true potential. He becomes aware of the need to develop a rich mindset—one that is open to abundance, opportunity, and wealth creation.

The Catalyst for Change: The awakening serves as a catalyst for John's transformation. He makes a commitment to himself and his family that he will do whatever it takes to change his financial situation. He understands that it won't be an overnight process, but he is willing to put in the effort, discipline, and dedication required to achieve his goals.

The Journey Begins: The chapter concludes with John's decision to embark on his journey towards financial success. He sets his sights on acquiring the knowledge, skills, and resources necessary to build wealth. John feels a renewed sense of purpose and determination, ready to overcome challenges and pursue a brighter future for himself and his loved ones.

"**The Awakening**" sets the stage for the rest of the book, establishing John's motivations, struggles, and newfound commitment to change. It highlights the pivotal moment when John realizes that he has the power to shape his financial destiny and sets him on a path towards acquiring the knowledge and skills needed to become the rich daddy he aspires to be.

CHAPTER 2

The Rich Mindset.

Exploring the importance of mindset in achieving financial success.

Introducing the concept of the "rich mindset" and its characteristics.

Sharing examples of successful individuals who have developed a rich mindset and transformed their lives.

Shifting Perspectives: The chapter begins by highlighting the need to shift perspectives and challenge limiting beliefs about money and wealth. It explores common societal narratives around scarcity, lack, and the idea that financial success is only attainable for a select few. It encourages readers to break free from these constraints and embrace a mindset that is open to possibilities and abundance.

Beliefs and Attitudes: The chapter examines the beliefs and attitudes that shape one's relationship with money. It emphasizes the significance of cultivating positive beliefs and attitudes towards wealth, such as seeing money as a tool for creating opportunities and making a positive impact in the world. It encourages readers to identify and transform any negative beliefs or attitudes that may be holding them back from achieving financial success.

Embracing Abundance: The rich mindset is centered around embracing abundance rather than scarcity. The chapter explores the idea that the universe is abundant and that there are limitless opportunities for wealth creation. It discusses the importance of adopting an abundance mindset, which involves cultivating gratitude, focusing on possibilities, and being open to receiving wealth and abundance.

Taking Responsibility: The rich mindset emphasizes personal responsibility and accountability for one's financial situation. It encourages readers to take ownership of their financial decisions, acknowledging that they have the power to shape their financial future. The chapter discusses the importance of avoiding a victim mentality and instead adopting an empowered mindset that embraces responsibility and proactive action.

Learning from Failure: Failure is a natural part of the journey towards financial success. The chapter highlights the rich mindset's approach to failure as an opportunity for growth and learning. It encourages readers to view setbacks as stepping stones towards success, to learn from mistakes, and to persevere in the face of challenges. It promotes a mindset that sees failure as feedback and as a catalyst for improvement and innovation.

Surrounding Yourself with Success: The chapter stresses the influence of the people we surround ourselves with. It emphasizes the importance of surrounding oneself with individuals who inspire, motivate, and support our financial goals. It explores the power of mentorship and the impact of being part of a network of like-minded individuals who can provide guidance, advice, and accountability.

Visualization and Affirmations: Visualizing success and using affirmations are powerful tools for developing a rich mindset. The chapter explores the practice of visualizing one's financial goals and creating a clear mental image of the desired outcomes. It also delves into the use of affirmations—positive statements that reinforce the belief in one's ability to achieve financial success.

Continuous Growth and Learning: The rich mindset recognizes that learning and personal growth are ongoing processes. The chapter encourages readers to embrace a mindset of continuous improvement, seeking knowledge, and expanding their skills in areas such as personal finance, investing, entrepreneurship, and wealth creation. It emphasizes the importance of staying curious, adaptable, and open to new ideas and opportunities.

CHAPTER 3

The roadmap to wealth.

**Discussing the importance of setting financial goals and creating a roadmap to achieve them.
The process of developing a comprehensive wealth plan, including budgeting, saving, investing, and managing debts.**

Providing practical tips and strategies for building wealth systematically.

Discussing the importance of setting financial goals and creating a roadmap to achieve them.

The process of developing a comprehensive wealth plan, including budgeting, saving, investing, and managing debts.

Providing practical tips and strategies for building wealth systematically.
Set Clear Goals: Start by defining your financial goals. Be specific about what you want to achieve, whether it's saving for retirement, buying a house, starting a business, or any other objective. Clear goals provide direction and motivation for your financial journey.

Create a Budget: Develop a detailed budget that outlines your income, expenses, and savings targets. A budget helps you track your spending, identify areas for improvement, and ensures that you're living within your means. Allocate funds for saving and investing to build wealth over time.

Build an Emergency Fund: Establish an emergency fund to cover unexpected expenses or financial setbacks. Aim to save three to six months' worth of living expenses in a readily accessible account. This fund acts as a safety net, allowing you to handle unforeseen circumstances without derailing your financial progress.

Reduce Debt: Prioritize reducing high-interest debts, such as credit card balances or personal loans. Make consistent payments above the minimum requirements to accelerate the payoff process. Consider debt consolidation or negotiation to lower interest rates and streamline your repayment efforts.

Save and Invest: Make saving a habit by allocating a portion of your income towards various investment vehicles. Start with low-risk options like savings accounts or certificates of deposit (CDs) to build a foundation. As you accumulate wealth, explore more diversified and higher-yielding investments, such as stocks, bonds, mutual funds, real estate, or starting your own business.

Diversify Investments: Spreading your investments across different asset classes helps mitigate risks and maximize returns. Consider a mix of stocks, bonds, real estate, and other investment vehicles that align with your risk tolerance and long-term objectives. Regularly review and rebalance your portfolio to maintain an optimal asset allocation.

Continual Learning: Educate yourself about personal finance, investing, and wealth-building strategies. Read books, attend seminars, follow reputable financial blogs or podcasts, and seek advice from financial professionals. Continuous learning helps you make informed decisions and adapt to changing economic conditions.

Maximize Income Potential: Look for opportunities to increase your income. This may involve advancing your career, acquiring new skills, pursuing higher education, starting a side business, or investing in income-generating assets. Aim to consistently grow your earnings over time.

Minimize Expenses: Be mindful of your spending habits and identify areas where you can reduce expenses. Differentiate between wants and needs, and make conscious choices to prioritize savings and investment contributions. Review your recurring bills, negotiate better rates, and avoid unnecessary purchases.

Estate Planning: As you accumulate wealth, consider estate planning to protect your assets and ensure their efficient transfer to future generations. Consult with professionals, such as estate lawyers or financial advisors, to create a comprehensive plan that includes wills, trusts, and other appropriate mechanisms.

Maintain Discipline and Patience: Wealth-building is a long-term endeavor that requires discipline and patience. Stick to your financial plan, avoid impulsive decisions, and remain committed to your goals even during market downturns or temporary setbacks. Stay focused on the big picture and adjust your strategy as needed, but avoid chasing quick gains or succumbing to market speculation.

CHAPTER 4

The Power of Passive Income.

Introducing the concept of passive income and its significance in achieving financial independence.

Exploring various passive income streams such as rental properties, dividend stocks, and online businesses.

Sharing success stories of individuals who have generated substantial passive income and achieved financial freedom.

Introduction: In this chapter, we will explore the concept of passive income and its significance in creating financial freedom and independence. Passive income refers to the earnings generated from assets or investments that require minimal effort or time to maintain. Unlike active income, which is earned through direct labor or services, passive income allows individuals to generate money even when they are not actively working. This chapter will delve into the various sources of passive income, its advantages, and how it can be leveraged to achieve long-term financial goals.

Understanding Passive Income:
Passive income is a key component of financial stability and wealth accumulation. It is often seen as a means to escape the traditional work routine and achieve financial freedom. Passive income streams can be generated through a variety of sources, including real estate investments, stock market dividends, rental properties, royalties from intellectual property, affiliate

marketing, online businesses, and more. The common thread among these sources is that they continue to generate income even when an individual is not actively involved in the day-to-day operations.Passive **Income:Financial Freedom**: Passive income provides a pathway to financial independence by creating a consistent cash flow that is not dependent on active labor. It allows individuals to have more control over their time and pursue other passions or endeavors.**Diversification**: Relying solely on active income from a job can be risky. Creating multiple streams of passive income diversifies one's earnings and reduces the vulnerability associated with relying on a single income source.Scalability: Passive income has the potential to be scaled up over time. By investing in assets or businesses that generate passive income, individuals can gradually increase their income streams and build substantial wealth in the long run. **Wealth**

Preservation: Passive income can act as a wealth preservation tool by creating a sustainable source of income that continues to generate returns even during retirement or periods of economic downturn.

Building Passive Income Streams:
Real Estate Investments: Investing in real estate properties, such as rental properties or commercial spaces, can generate passive income through rental payments. Real estate investments offer both monthly cash flow and long-term appreciation potential. **Dividend Stocks**: Dividend stocks are shares of companies that distribute a portion of their earnings to shareholders. By investing in dividend-paying stocks, individuals can receive regular dividend payments, which constitute passive income. **Online Businesses**: The digital age has opened up various opportunities for creating passive income through online businesses. These can include e-commerce

stores, affiliate marketing websites, online courses, or even content creation platforms. Intellectual Property: Intellectual property, such as books, music, patents, or trademarks, can generate passive income through royalties. This income is earned whenever the intellectual property is used or sold.

Achieving Passive Income Success: Research and Education: It is crucial to gain knowledge about different passive income strategies and the specific industries or assets in which you plan to invest. Conduct thorough research, attend seminars, read books, and learn from experts who have successfully built passive income streams.Patience and Persistence: Building passive income takes time and effort. It requires patience to research, analyze opportunities, and make sound investment decisions. Persistence is also vital when facing challenges or setbacks along the way.

Risk Management: While passive income can be rewarding, it is essential to assess and manage risks effectively. Diversification, conducting due diligence, and seeking professional advice can help mitigate potential risks. **Active Monitoring and Adaptation:** Although passive income is designed to require minimal effort, it is important to actively monitor and manage your income streams.

CHAPTER 5

The art of investing.

Understanding the basics of investing and its role in wealth creation.

Explaining different investment vehicles such as stocks, bonds, real estate, and mutual funds.

Highlighting key investment principles and strategies to maximize returns while minimizing risks.

The art of investing is a multifaceted discipline that involves the strategic allocation of financial resources with the goal of generating returns and preserving capital over time. Successful investing requires a combination of knowledge, skill, patience, and discipline. In this response, we'll explore the key principles and strategies associated with the art of investing.

Goal Setting: The first step in investing is to define your financial goals. Whether it's saving for retirement, buying a house, funding your children's education, or achieving financial independence, having clear goals helps shape your investment strategy.

Risk Assessment: Assessing your risk tolerance is crucial in determining the types of investments that align with your comfort level. Risk and return are typically related, with higher-risk investments potentially offering higher returns but also greater volatility and potential losses.

Diversification: The saying "don't put all your eggs in one basket" applies to investing as well. Diversification involves spreading your investments across different asset classes (e.g., stocks, bonds, real estate) and within each asset class to reduce the impact of a single investment's performance on your overall portfolio. Diversification helps mitigate risk and capture potential gains from various sources.

Asset Allocation: Asset allocation involves determining the optimal mix of asset classes in your portfolio based on your goals, risk tolerance, and investment time horizon. A well-diversified portfolio typically includes a mix of stocks, bonds, cash, and potentially alternative investments.

Fundamental Analysis: Fundamental analysis is the process of evaluating the intrinsic value of an investment by examining its financial statements, competitive position, industry trends, management team, and other relevant factors. This analysis helps investors identify undervalued or overvalued assets and make informed investment decisions.

Technical Analysis: Technical analysis involves studying historical price and volume patterns to identify trends and forecast future price movements. This approach relies on charts, indicators, and statistical models to determine entry and exit points. Technical analysis is commonly used in short-term trading strategies.

Long-Term Perspective: Successful investing requires a long-term perspective. The market goes through cycles, and short-term fluctuations can be influenced by various factors, including market sentiment and economic conditions. By maintaining a long-term view, investors can ride out market volatility and potentially benefit from compounding returns over time.

Risk Management: Managing risk is a crucial aspect of investing. This includes setting stop-loss orders to limit potential losses, having an emergency fund to handle unforeseen expenses, and periodically reviewing and rebalancing your portfolio to ensure it aligns with your risk tolerance and investment objectives.

Continuous Learning: Investing is a dynamic field, and staying informed about market trends, economic developments, and new investment opportunities is essential. Continuously educating yourself through books, financial news, seminars, or working with a financial advisor can enhance your investing skills.

Emotional Discipline: Emotions can often cloud judgment when it comes to investing. Fear and greed are common emotional pitfalls that can lead to irrational investment decisions. Developing emotional discipline and sticking to your investment strategy, even during market downturns or euphoric periods, is vital for long-term success.

It's important to note that investing involves risks, and past performance is not indicative of future results. It's recommended to consult with a qualified financial advisor or conduct thorough research before making investment decisions. The art of investing requires a blend of knowledge, experience, and a willingness to adapt to changing market conditions while staying focused on long-term goals.

CHAPTER 6

The entrepreneurial spirit.

Exploring the world of entrepreneurship and its potential for wealth generation.

Discussing the mindset and qualities required to become a successful entrepreneur.

Sharing inspiring stories of entrepreneurs who started from scratch and built thriving businesses.

The entrepreneurial spirit refers to a set of characteristics, mindset, and attitude that drives individuals to identify and pursue opportunities for innovation, creation, and business ventures. It embodies the willingness to take risks, the ability to think creatively, and the determination to overcome challenges in order to achieve success. The entrepreneurial spirit is often associated with entrepreneurs, business founders, and individuals who start and manage their own enterprises, but it can also be found in intrapreneurs within larger organizations.

Here are some key aspects that define the entrepreneurial spirit:

Opportunity Recognition:
Entrepreneurs have a keen ability to identify opportunities that others may overlook. They are observant, innovative, and have a knack for identifying gaps in the market or emerging trends that can be turned into successful business ventures. They constantly seek new possibilities and are willing to challenge the status quo.

Risk-Taking: Entrepreneurs are comfortable with taking calculated risks.

They understand that starting a business involves uncertainty and are willing to invest their time, energy, and resources into ventures that have the potential for significant rewards. They are not afraid of failure and view it as a learning opportunity rather than a setback.

Creativity and Innovation: The entrepreneurial spirit thrives on creativity and innovation. Entrepreneurs are adept at thinking outside the box, finding novel solutions to problems, and introducing disruptive ideas or products to the market. They are open-minded and embrace change as an opportunity for growth and improvement.

Self-Confidence and Self-Motivation: Entrepreneurs possess a strong sense of self-confidence and belief in their abilities. They are driven by their passion and have a clear vision of what they want to achieve.

They are self-motivated and do not rely on external validation or rewards to keep pushing forward in the face of obstacles or setbacks.

Adaptability and Resilience:
Entrepreneurs understand that the business landscape is constantly evolving, and they need to adapt quickly to changes. They are resilient in the face of challenges and setbacks, and they view failures as valuable learning experiences. They are flexible and willing to pivot their strategies or ideas when necessary to stay ahead of the competition.

Networking and Relationship-Building: Entrepreneurs recognize the importance of building a strong network of connections. They actively seek opportunities to network with like-minded individuals, mentors, investors, and potential customers. They understand that strong relationships can provide valuable support, advice, and collaboration opportunities.

Persistence and Determination: Entrepreneurship is often a long and challenging journey, and entrepreneurs need to have a high level of persistence and determination. They are willing to work hard, put in long hours, and make sacrifices to achieve their goals. They do not give up easily and remain committed to their vision, even in the face of adversity.The entrepreneurial spirit is not limited to a specific industry or field. It can be found in various sectors, such as technology, healthcare, finance, and social entrepreneurship. It drives individuals to turn ideas into reality, create value for themselves and society, and contribute to economic growth and innovation.

In conclusion, the entrepreneurial spirit encompasses a combination of traits, behaviors, and attitudes that enable individuals to identify opportunities, take risks, think creatively, and persistently pursue their goals. It is a driving force behind entrepreneurship and fosters a culture of innovation and growth.

CHAPTER 7

The importance of financial education.

Emphasizing the significance of financial education in achieving long-term financial success.

Discussing the shortcomings of traditional education systems in teaching financial literacy.

Providing resources and strategies to enhance financial knowledge and empower readers to make informed financial decisions.

Financial education is crucial for individuals at all income levels, including those with significant wealth, often referred to as a "rich daddy." While one might assume that individuals with substantial financial resources do not require financial education, the reality is quite different. Here, we'll discuss in detail the importance of financial education for a rich daddy.

Wealth preservation: A rich daddy must focus on preserving and growing their wealth. Financial education equips them with the necessary knowledge and skills to make informed investment decisions, manage risks effectively, and protect their assets. It helps them understand complex financial instruments, tax strategies, estate planning, and other essential aspects of wealth management.

Smart investment decisions: Financial education enables a rich daddy to make intelligent investment choices. It equips them with a deeper understanding of different investment vehicles, such as stocks, bonds, real estate, mutual funds, and private equity. They can analyze investment opportunities, evaluate risks and potential returns, and make informed decisions aligned with their financial goals.

Diversification: Financial education emphasizes the importance of diversifying one's investment portfolio. It helps a rich daddy understand the benefits of spreading investments across various asset classes, sectors, and geographies. By diversifying, they can reduce risks and protect their wealth from substantial losses that may occur in a single investment.

Entrepreneurship and business ventures: Financial education can inspire and guide a rich daddy who wishes to engage in entrepreneurship or start a business venture. It teaches them about business finance, budgeting, cash flow management, and risk assessment. They can develop skills in strategic planning, marketing, and financial analysis, increasing their chances of success in their entrepreneurial endeavors.

Philanthropy and legacy planning: Many affluent individuals aspire to give back to society and leave a lasting impact through philanthropy. Financial education helps a rich daddy understand how they can align their wealth with their philanthropic goals effectively. It assists in developing charitable giving strategies, establishing foundations or trusts, and optimizing their contributions to make a meaningful difference.

Family wealth management: Rich daddies often have a responsibility to pass on their wealth to future generations. Financial education equips them with the knowledge and tools necessary to educate their children about financial literacy and responsible wealth management. They can instill important values such as fiscal responsibility, saving habits, and wise investment decisions in their heirs, ensuring the preservation of family wealth.

Protection against financial fraud: Financial education also serves as a defense against scams, frauds, and unethical financial practices that can target wealthy individuals. It helps a rich daddy recognize warning signs, identify fraudulent schemes, and protect their assets from potential harm. By understanding the intricacies of the financial landscape, they can make informed choices and avoid falling victim to fraudulent activities.

In summary, financial education plays a crucial role in the life of a rich daddy. It empowers them to make informed decisions, preserve and grow their wealth, navigate complex financial landscapes, and make a positive impact through philanthropy. By continually expanding their financial knowledge and skills, rich daddies can secure their financial future and contribute to the well-being of their families, communities, and society as a whole.

CHAPTER 8

The role of networking and mentorship.

Highlighting the importance of building a strong network and seeking guidance from mentors.

Discussing how networking and mentorship can open doors to opportunities and accelerate personal growth.

Sharing practical tips for networking effectively and finding suitable mentors in different areas of life.

Networking and mentorship can play significant roles in an individual's personal and professional development, and having a rich daddy can potentially provide unique opportunities and advantages in these areas. Let's discuss each aspect in detail:

Networking:
Networking refers to the process of establishing and nurturing relationships with individuals who share similar interests, goals, or professional backgrounds. It involves building a network of contacts that can offer support, guidance, and potential opportunities.

When someone has a rich daddy, they often have access to a wide range of influential and successful people within their social circle. This access can open doors to various opportunities that may not be readily available to others. For example, a rich daddy may have connections with influential business leaders, politicians, or industry professionals who can provide valuable insights, introductions, or even job opportunities.

Networking through a rich daddy's connections can accelerate an individual's access to resources, information, and opportunities. These connections can help in securing internships, scholarships, job placements, or business partnerships that might otherwise be challenging to obtain. Networking with successful individuals also allows for exposure to different perspectives, knowledge, and experiences, enabling personal and professional growth.

However, it's important to note that networking solely based on the wealth or status of a rich daddy may not be sustainable or meaningful in the long run. Building genuine relationships and demonstrating one's own skills, expertise, and character is crucial to making lasting connections. It's essential to utilize the opportunities provided by a rich daddy's network while also developing one's own networking skills and expanding contacts beyond the initial advantage.

Mentorship:
Mentorship involves a partnership between a more experienced individual (mentor) and a less experienced individual (mentee), where the mentor provides guidance, advice, and support to the mentee's personal and professional growth.

Having a rich daddy as a mentor can provide numerous advantages. A wealthy and successful parent can offer insights into their own experiences, achievements, and failures, providing valuable lessons and perspectives. They may have built successful businesses or established careers in specific industries, making them a valuable source of knowledge and expertise.

A rich daddy's mentorship can involve various aspects, such as:

Financial Education: A wealthy parent can provide guidance on managing finances, investment strategies, and wealth preservation. They can impart knowledge about personal finance, budgeting, and strategies for wealth accumulation.

Business and Career Advice: If the rich daddy is an entrepreneur or has expertise in a particular field, they can offer insights into business strategies, industry trends, and career development. This guidance can be invaluable when starting a business, pursuing a specific career path, or making important professional decisions.

Access to Resources: A rich daddy can provide access to resources such as capital, connections, or specialized knowledge that can significantly benefit a mentee's endeavors. For instance, they may fund business ventures, introduce the mentee to influential contacts, or offer access to exclusive events or opportunities.

However, it's important for both the mentor and the mentee to establish clear boundaries and expectations within the mentorship relationship. It should be a mutually beneficial arrangement where the mentee actively seeks guidance, demonstrates initiative, and takes responsibility for their own growth. It's crucial for the mentee to develop their own skills, capabilities, and network beyond the advantages provided by their rich daddy.

In conclusion, the role of networking and mentorship in the context of having a rich daddy can be influential. Networking through a wealthy parent's connections can offer unique opportunities and access to influential individuals. Mentorship from a rich daddy can provide valuable guidance, insights, and resources for personal and professional growth. However, it's essential to balance these advantages with developing one's own skills, capabilities, and network, ensuring a sustainable path to success independent of external factors.

CHAPTER 9

The Legacy of Wealth.

Discussing the significance of leaving a financial legacy for future generations.

Exploring estate planning, wills, trusts, and other tools for wealth preservation.

Sharing stories of individuals who have successfully passed on their wealth and values to their heirs.

"The Legacy of Wealth" refers to the long-lasting impact and influence of the book "Rich Dad Poor Dad" by **DANNY J.BAYS**. Published in 2023, this book became an international bestseller and had a significant impact on the personal finance and self-help genres. It presents valuable lessons and insights into building wealth and achieving financial independence.

One of the key legacies of "Rich Dad Poor Dad" is its ability to challenge conventional wisdom about money and financial success. Kiyosaki shares his own personal experiences and contrasts the mindsets of his two fathers: his real father (poor dad), who had a traditional approach to money, and his friend's father (rich dad), who had a more entrepreneurial and wealth-building mindset. By questioning traditional beliefs and providing alternative perspectives, the book encourages readers to think critically about their financial decisions and consider alternative paths to success.

Another significant aspect of the book's legacy is its emphasis on financial education.the traditional education system often fails to teach essential financial literacy skills, leaving individuals ill-prepared to navigate the complexities of money management and wealth creation. He advocates for self-education and gaining a deep understanding of concepts such as assets, liabilities, cash flow, and investing. This message has resonated with readers worldwide, leading to increased interest in financial education and the development of numerous resources and programs aimed at improving financial literacy.

"Rich Dad Poor Dad" also popularized the concept of passive income and introduced the idea of using assets to generate ongoing cash flow. I encourages readers to shift their focus from relying solely on earned income (salary or wages) to building assets that generate passive income, such as real estate investments, stocks, and businesses. This concept has inspired many individuals to explore different avenues for generating income beyond traditional employment and to seek financial independence.

Furthermore, the book's legacy lies in its motivational aspect. Kiyosaki shares his personal journey from financial struggles to financial success, offering inspiration and encouragement to readers who aspire to improve their financial situations. By sharing anecdotes and stories, the book fosters a mindset of possibility and encourages readers to take action, overcome obstacles, and strive for their financial goals.

The legacy of "Rich Dad Poor Dad" can also be seen in the proliferation of subsequent books, seminars, and educational materials that have built upon its principles. Kiyosaki himself has authored numerous follow-up books, expanding on the original concepts and providing more detailed guidance on wealth creation and financial intelligence. Additionally, the book has influenced and inspired a generation of authors, speakers, and entrepreneurs who have built their own platforms and teachings around financial literacy and wealth creation.

However, it's worth noting that the book has received criticism as well. Some argue that Kiyosaki's advice is oversimplified or lacks practicality, while others question the credibility of the author's personal experiences and financial claims. Nonetheless, the book's enduring popularity and the impact it has had on millions of readers worldwide are undeniable.

In conclusion, the legacy of "Rich Dad Poor Dad" is multifaceted. It challenges traditional financial beliefs, promotes financial education, introduces the concept of passive income, motivates readers to take action, and has spawned a wealth of subsequent resources and teachings. Whether one agrees or disagrees with its principles, the book has undoubtedly left a lasting mark on the personal finance landscape and continues to influence individuals seeking to improve their financial well-being.

CHAPTER 10

The Balanced wealth.

The concept of the "balanced wealth of a rich daddy" refers to the notion that a wealthy individual, particularly a parent, should not only focus on accumulating financial wealth but also on instilling other forms of wealth, such as values, education, and experiences, in their children. It emphasizes the importance of a well-rounded approach to wealth that goes beyond monetary assets.

When discussing the balanced wealth of a rich daddy, it's crucial to consider various aspects that contribute to a holistic and fulfilling life. Here are some key elements to explore:

Financial Wealth: Undoubtedly, financial wealth plays a significant role in providing security and opportunities for oneself and future generations. A rich daddy may amass substantial financial resources through successful entrepreneurship, investments, or inheritance. However, the concept of balanced wealth suggests that focusing solely on money can neglect other essential aspects of life.

Values and Character Development: A rich daddy should prioritize imparting strong values, ethics, and character development to their children. This involves teaching them virtues like honesty, empathy, responsibility, and gratitude. By instilling these values, a rich daddy ensures that their children are not solely defined by their financial status but also by their integrity and how they contribute positively to society.

Education and Intellectual Wealth: Providing a quality education for children is vital for their personal and intellectual growth. A rich daddy can invest in their children's education, ensuring they have access to excellent schools, tutors, and extracurricular activities. This investment in intellectual wealth empowers children to develop critical thinking skills, broaden their knowledge, and pursue their passions.

Emotional and Mental Well-being: The balanced wealth of a rich daddy also considers the emotional and mental well-being of their children. It involves fostering a supportive and nurturing environment, offering guidance, and promoting open communication. Encouraging healthy relationships, emotional intelligence, and resilience equips children with the tools to navigate life's challenges and maintain overall well-being.

Experiences and Personal Growth:
Wealthy individuals have the opportunity to provide enriching experiences to their children. These experiences can include travel, cultural exploration, philanthropic endeavors, and exposure to diverse perspectives. Such experiences broaden children's horizons, promote personal growth, and cultivate a sense of empathy and global awareness.

The concept of balanced wealth encourages rich daddies to think beyond their immediate family and consider their legacy. Philanthropy and giving back to society can be an integral part of their wealth strategy. By engaging in charitable endeavors, they can make a positive impact on causes they care about, leaving a lasting legacy that extends beyond material possessions.

In summary, the balanced wealth of a rich daddy encompasses more than just financial riches. It involves a comprehensive approach that considers values, education, emotional well-being, experiences, personal growth, and a commitment to making a positive impact. By nurturing these various forms of wealth, a rich daddy can help their children lead fulfilling lives and create a lasting legacy that extends beyond monetary assets.